· SPLENDID ·

Sweet Potato

RECIPES

BRUNCHES, DINNERS, SIDES, AND DESSERTS

D1308133

pil

Publications International, Ltd.

Microwave Cooking: Microwave ovens vary in wattage. Use the cooking times as guidelines and check for doneness before adding more time.

CONTENTS

BREAKFAST & BRUNCH

Sweet Potato and Turkey Sausage Hash

—— Makes 2 to 4 servings ——

- 1 red onion
- 1 red bell pepper
- 1 sweet potato, peeled
- 2 mild or hot turkey Italian sausage links (about 4 ounces each)

- ½ teaspoon salt
- ¼ teaspoon black pepper
- ⅛ teaspoon ground cumin
- ⅛ teaspoon chipotle chili powder

1. Use a spiral cutter to cut vegetables into desired lengths.*

2. Remove sausage from casings; shape sausage into ½-inch balls. Spray large nonstick skillet with nonstick cooking spray; heat over medium heat. Add sausage; cook and stir 3 to 5 minutes or until browned. Remove from skillet; set aside.

3. Spray same skillet with cooking spray. Add onion, bell pepper, sweet potato, salt, black pepper, cumin and chili powder; cook and stir 5 to 8 minutes or until sweet potato is tender.

4. Stir in sausage; cook, without stirring, 5 minutes or until hash is lightly browned.

If you don't have a spiral cutter, you can also chop or finely dice the vegetables.

Sweet Potato Muffins

—— Makes 24 muffins ——

2 cups all-purpose flour
¾ cup chopped walnuts
¾ cup golden raisins
½ cup packed brown sugar
1 tablespoon baking powder
1 teaspoon ground cinnamon
½ teaspoon salt

½ teaspoon baking soda
¼ teaspoon ground nutmeg
1 cup mashed cooked sweet potato
¾ cup milk
½ cup (1 stick) butter, melted
2 eggs, beaten
1½ teaspoons vanilla

1. Preheat oven to 400°F. Grease 24 standard (2½-inch) muffin cups.

2. Combine flour, walnuts, raisins, brown sugar, baking powder, cinnamon, salt, baking soda and nutmeg in medium bowl; stir until well blended.

3. Combine sweet potato, milk, butter, eggs and vanilla in large bowl; stir until well blended. Add flour mixture to sweet potato mixture; stir just until moistened. Spoon batter evenly into prepared muffin cups.

4. Bake 15 minutes or until toothpick inserted into centers comes out clean. Cool in pans 5 minutes. Remove to wire racks; cool completely.

Sweet and Savory
Sausage Casserole
— Makes 4 to 6 servings —

2 sweet potatoes, peeled and cut into 1-inch cubes

2 apples, peeled, cored and cut into 1-inch cubes

1 onion, cut into thin strips

2 tablespoons vegetable oil

2 teaspoons Italian seasoning

1 teaspoon garlic powder

½ teaspoon salt

½ teaspoon black pepper

1 pound Italian sausage, cooked and cut into ½-inch pieces

1. Preheat oven to 400°F. Lightly spray 13×9-inch baking dish with nonstick cooking spray.

2. Combine sweet potatoes, apples, onion, oil, Italian seasoning, garlic powder, salt and pepper in large bowl; toss to coat evenly. Transfer to prepared baking dish.

3. Cover and bake 30 minutes. Add sausage; bake, covered, 10 minutes or until sausage is heated through and sweet potatoes are tender.

Sweet Potato Biscuits

—————— Makes 12 rolls ——————

1½ cups all-purpose flour, plus additional for work surface

2 tablespoons packed dark brown sugar

1 tablespoon baking powder

½ teaspoon salt

½ teaspoon ground cinnamon

⅛ teaspoon ground nutmeg

5 tablespoons unsalted butter, cut into small pieces

1 cold puréed cooked sweet potato (about 1 large sweet potato)

½ cup low-fat buttermilk

2 tablespoons honey

1. Preheat oven to 450°F. Spray baking sheet with nonstick cooking spray.

2. Combine 1½ cups flour, brown sugar, baking powder, salt, cinnamon and nutmeg in medium bowl; mix well. Cut in butter with pastry blender or two knives until coarse crumbs form. Stir in sweet potato and buttermilk until combined.

3. Transfer dough to floured work surface. Using floured hands, knead dough five times or until no longer sticky, adding additional flour if necessary. Pat dough into ¼-inch thick disc. Cut out dough with 2½-inch round cutter. Reroll scraps and cut out additional pieces. Place 1 inch apart on prepared baking sheet. Refrigerate 20 minutes.

4. Bake 12 to 14 minutes or until biscuits are light golden brown and puffed. Immediately brush tops evenly with honey. Remove to wire racks; cool 5 minutes. Serve warm.

Sweet Potato Pancakes with Apple-Cherry Chutney

—— Makes 6 servings ——

Apple-Cherry Chutney
(recipe follows)

1 pound sweet potatoes
(about 2 medium), peeled

½ small onion

3 egg whites

2 tablespoons all-purpose flour

½ teaspoon salt

¼ teaspoon black pepper

4 teaspoons vegetable oil,
divided

1. Prepare Apple-Cherry Chutney; set aside.

2. Cut sweet potatoes into chunks. Combine sweet potatoes, onion, egg whites, flour, salt and pepper in food processor or blender; process until almost smooth (mixture will appear grainy).

3. Heat large nonstick skillet over medium heat 1 minute. Add 1 teaspoon oil. Spoon ⅓ cup batter per pancake into skillet. Cook 3 pancakes at a time, 3 minutes per side or until golden brown. Repeat with remaining oil and batter. Serve with Apple-Cherry Chutney.

Apple-Cherry Chutney

1 cup chunky applesauce

½ cup canned tart red cherries, drained

2 tablespoons sucralose-based sugar substitute

1 teaspoon lemon juice

½ teaspoon ground cinnamon

⅛ teaspoon ground nutmeg

Combine all ingredients in small saucepan; bring to a boil. Reduce heat; simmer 5 minutes. Serve warm.

Sweet Potato Casserole with Sweet Oat and Coconut Topping

Makes 8 servings

6 cups water

1¾ pounds sweet potatoes, peeled and cut into 1-inch cubes

½ cup pourable sugar substitute*

2 teaspoons ground cinnamon

½ teaspoon ground nutmeg

⅛ teaspoon salt (optional)

¼ cup cholesterol-free egg substitute

¼ cup reduced-fat margarine

2 teaspoons vanilla

Topping

¼ cup quick-cooking oats

⅓ cup flaked coconut

1½ ounces pecan chips (about ⅓ cup total)

3 tablespoons maple syrup

This recipe was tested using sucralose-based sugar substitute.

1. Preheat oven to 325°F. Bring water to a boil in large saucepan over high heat. Add sweet potatoes, return to a boil; reduce heat. Cover and simmer 18 to 20 minutes or until very tender when pierced with fork. Drain in colander, shaking off excess liquid.

2. Meanwhile, in small bowl combine topping ingredients, except maple syrup. Set aside.

3. Place sweet potatoes in large bowl. Using an electric mixer on medium-high speed, beat until smooth. Add sugar substitute, cinnamon, nutmeg, salt, if desired, egg substitute, margarine and vanilla. Beat on medium speed until smooth.

4. Coat 9-inch glass deep-dish pie pan with nonstick cooking spray. Spoon sweet potato mixture into pan. Sprinkle oat mixture evenly over all. Bake 35 minutes or until lightly browned.

5. To serve, drizzle maple syrup evenly over all.

DINNER WINNERS

Sweet Potato Bisque

—— Makes 4 servings ——

1 pound sweet potatoes, peeled and cut into 2-inch pieces
2 teaspoons butter
½ cup finely chopped onion
1 teaspoon curry powder
½ teaspoon ground coriander

¼ teaspoon salt
⅔ cup unsweetened apple juice
1 cup buttermilk
¼ cup water (optional)
Chopped fresh chives (optional)

1. Place sweet potatoes in large saucepan; add enough water to cover. Bring to a boil over high heat. Cook 15 minutes or until potatoes are fork-tender. Drain; cool under cold running water.

2. Meanwhile, melt butter in small saucepan over medium heat. Add onion; cook and stir 2 minutes. Stir in curry powder, coriander and salt; cook and stir 1 minute or until onion is tender. Remove from heat; stir in apple juice.

3. Combine sweet potatoes, buttermilk and onion mixture in food processor or blender; cover and process until smooth. Return to saucepan; stir in water, if necessary to thin to desired consistency. Cook and stir over medium heat until heated through. *Do not boil.* Garnish with chives.

Zucchini and Sweet Potato Stuffed Peppers

— Makes 4 servings —

4 red bell peppers (about 6 ounces each)

2 teaspoons olive oil

1 medium zucchini, diced

1 small onion, diced

½ cup diced celery

1 teaspoon Italian seasoning

½ teaspoon salt (optional)

¼ teaspoon black pepper

1 sweet potato, peeled and diced

¼ cup vegetable broth

2 tablespoons toasted pine nuts*

To toast pine nuts, spread in single layer in heavy skillet. Cook over medium heat 1 to 2 minutes or until nuts are lightly browned, stirring frequently.

1. Preheat oven to 375°F. Spray baking dish with nonstick cooking spray.

2. Slice tops off bell peppers; remove seeds and membranes. Bring large pot of water to a boil. Add bell peppers; cover and cook 5 minutes or until bell peppers start to soften. Remove with tongs; drain upside down.

3. Heat oil in large skillet over medium-high heat. Add zucchini, onion, celery, Italian seasoning, salt, if desired, and black pepper; cook 5 to 7 minutes or until zucchini is browned and vegetables are tender, stirring occasionally. Add sweet potatoes during last 3 minutes of cooking. Reduce heat if browning too quickly.

4. Combine vegetable mixture, broth and pine nuts in large bowl; spoon into bell peppers. Transfer to prepared baking dish. Bake 15 minutes or until sweet potatoes are tender and filling is heated through.

Bean and Vegetable Burritos

Makes 4 servings

2 tablespoons chili powder

2 teaspoons dried oregano

1½ teaspoons ground cumin

1 large sweet potato, diced

1 can (about 15 ounces) black or pinto beans, rinsed and drained

4 cloves garlic, minced

1 medium onion, halved and thinly sliced

1 jalapeño pepper,* seeded and minced

1 green bell pepper, chopped

1 cup frozen corn, thawed and drained

3 tablespoons lime juice

1 tablespoon chopped fresh cilantro

¾ cup (3 ounces) shredded Monterey Jack cheese

4 (10-inch) flour tortillas

Sour cream (optional)

Jalapeño peppers can sting and irritate the skin, so wear rubber gloves when handling peppers and do not touch your eyes.

Slow Cooker Directions

1. Combine chili powder, oregano and cumin in small bowl. Set aside.

2. Layer ingredients in slow cooker in the following order: sweet potato, beans, half of chili powder mixture, garlic, onion, jalapeño pepper, bell pepper, remaining half of chili powder mixture and corn. Cover; cook on LOW 5 hours or until sweet potato is tender. Stir in lime juice and cilantro.

3. Preheat oven to 350°F. Spoon about 2 tablespoons cheese in center of each tortilla. Top with 1 cup filling. Fold two sides over filling and roll up. Place burritos, seam side down, on baking sheet. Cover with foil and bake 20 to 30 minutes or until heated through. Serve with sour cream, if desired.

Asian Sweet Potato and Corn Stew

— Makes 6 servings —

1 tablespoon vegetable oil

1 large onion, chopped

2 tablespoons peeled and minced fresh ginger

½ jalapeño or serrano pepper,* seeded and minced

2 cloves garlic, minced

1 cup drained canned or thawed frozen corn kernels

2 teaspoons curry powder

1 can (13½ ounces) coconut milk, well shaken

1 teaspoon cornstarch

1 can (about 14 ounces) vegetable broth

1 tablespoon soy sauce, plus more to taste

4 sweet potatoes, peeled and cut into ¾-inch cubes

Hot cooked jasmine or long-grain rice

Chopped fresh cilantro (optional)

Jalapeño and serrano peppers can sting and irritate the skin, so wear rubber gloves when handling peppers and do not touch your eyes.

Slow Cooker Directions

1. Heat oil in large skillet over medium heat. Add onion, ginger, minced jalapeño pepper and garlic. Cook about 5 minutes, stirring occasionally, or until onion softens. Remove from heat; stir in drained corn and curry powder.

2. Whisk coconut milk and cornstarch together in slow cooker. Stir in broth and soy sauce. Carefully add sweet potatoes; top with curried corn. Cover; cook on LOW 5 to 6 hours or until sweet potatoes are tender. Stir gently to smooth cooking liquid (coconut milk may look curdled) without breaking up sweet potatoes. Adjust seasoning to taste with additional soy sauce. Spoon over rice in serving bowls and sprinkle with cilantro, if desired.

Serving Suggestion: Garnish with coarsely chopped dry-roasted peanuts and chopped green onions for extra flavor and crunch.

Maple Salmon and Sweets

Makes 4 servings

½ cup pure maple syrup
2 tablespoons butter, melted
1½ pounds skin-on salmon fillets
2 medium sweet potatoes, peeled and cut into ¼-inch slices

1 teaspoon salt
¼ teaspoon black pepper

1. Combine maple syrup and butter in small bowl. Place salmon in large resealable food storage bag. Place sweet potatoes in another large resealable food storage bag. Pour half of syrup mixture into each bag; seal. Refrigerate at least 2 hours or overnight, turning bags occasionally.

2. Prepare grill for direct cooking. Oil grid. Drain salmon and sweet potatoes; discard marinade. Season with salt and pepper.

3. Grill salmon, skin-side down, on covered grill over medium heat 15 to 20 minutes or until fish begins to flake when tested with fork. (*Do not turn.*) Grill sweet potatoes, covered, in single layer on grill topper 15 minutes or until tender and slightly browned, turning once or twice or until tender and slightly browned.

Chicken and Sweet Potato Chili

Makes 4 servings

1 to 2 sweet potatoes, peeled and cut into ½-inch chunks

2 teaspoons canola oil

1 cup chopped onion

¾ pound boneless skinless chicken breasts or chicken tenders, cut into ¾-inch chunks*

3 cloves garlic, minced

2 teaspoons chili powder

1 can (about 14 ounces) diced fire-roasted tomatoes, undrained

1 can (about 15 ounces) no-salt-added kidney beans or pinto beans, drained

½ cup chipotle or jalapeño salsa

This is easier to do if chicken is partially frozen.

1. Place sweet potatoes in large saucepan and add enough water to cover. Bring to a boil. Reduce heat; simmer 5 minutes or until almost tender. Drain sweet potatoes; set aside. Heat oil in large saucepan over medium heat. Add onion; cook and stir 5 minutes.

2. Add chicken, garlic and chili powder; cook 3 minutes, stirring frequently. Add tomatoes, beans, salsa and sweet potatoes; bring to a boil over high heat. Reduce heat; simmer uncovered 10 minutes or until chicken is cooked through.

Sweet Potato Shepherd's Pie

—————— Makes 6 servings ——————

1 large sweet potato, peeled and cubed

1 large russet potato, peeled and cubed

½ to 1 cup milk

1½ teaspoons salt, divided

2 cups chicken broth

3 tablespoons all-purpose flour

1 teaspoon cider vinegar

1 teaspoon dried thyme

½ teaspoon dried sage

½ teaspoon black pepper

1 pound ground turkey

2 packages (4 ounces each) sliced mixed mushrooms *or* 8 ounces sliced cremini mushrooms

1 tablespoon minced garlic

¾ cup frozen baby peas, thawed

1. Place potatoes in medium saucepan. Cover with water; bring to a boil over medium-high heat. Reduce heat; cover and simmer 20 minutes or until potatoes are very tender. Drain potatoes; return to saucepan. Mash with potato masher; stir in enough milk until desired consistency is reached and ½ teaspoon salt.

2. Heat broth in small saucepan over medium heat. Whisk in flour; cook and stir 2 minutes. Reduce heat to low; cook until thickened. Stir in vinegar, thyme, remaining 1 teaspoon salt, sage and pepper.

3. Spray large nonstick ovenproof skillet with nonstick cooking spray. Add turkey, mushrooms and garlic; cook and stir over medium-high heat until turkey is no longer pink and mushrooms begin to give off liquid.

4. Pour gravy into skillet; simmer 5 minutes. Add peas; cook and stir until heated through. Remove from heat. Spoon potato mixture over turkey mixture; spray with cooking spray.

5. Preheat broiler. Broil 4 to 5 inches from heat source 5 minutes or until mixture is heated through and potatoes begin to brown.

Hip Hop Hash

— Makes 4 servings —

1 tablespoon butter

1 tablespoon sweet rice flour (mochiko)

⅓ cup beef broth

1 teaspoon Worcestershire sauce

1 pound beef pot roast, cooked and diced

1 medium sweet potato (about 12 ounces), peeled and diced

1 stalk celery, diced

1 cup corn

¼ cup diced red or green bell pepper

¼ cup (1 ounce) shredded Cheddar cheese (optional)

1. Melt butter in large skillet over medium heat. Whisk in sweet rice flour; cook 2 minutes, stirring constantly. Whisk in broth and Worcestershire sauce; bring to a simmer. Add beef, sweet potato, celery, corn and bell pepper. Return to a simmer; cover and cook 12 minutes or until vegetables are tender.

2. Sprinkle cheese over hash just before serving, if desired.

Pork and Sweet Potato Skillet

———— Makes 4 servings ————

¾ **pound pork tenderloin, cut into 1-inch cubes**

1 **tablespoon plus 1 teaspoon butter, divided**

¼ **teaspoon salt**

⅛ **teaspoon black pepper**

2 **medium sweet potatoes, peeled and cut into ½-inch pieces (about 2 cups)**

1 **small onion, sliced**

¼ **pound reduced-fat smoked turkey sausage, halved lengthwise and cut into ½-inch pieces**

1 **small green or red apple, cut into ½-inch slices**

½ **cup sweet and sour sauce**

2 **tablespoons chopped fresh parsley (optional)**

1. Place pork and 1 teaspoon butter in large nonstick skillet; cook and stir 2 to 3 minutes over medium-high heat or until pork is no longer pink. Season with salt and pepper. Remove from skillet.

2. Add remaining 1 tablespoon butter, sweet potatoes and onion to skillet. Cover; cook and stir over medium-low heat 8 to 10 minutes or until tender.

3. Add pork, sausage, apple and sweet and sour sauce to skillet; cook and stir until heated through. Garnish with parsley.

Tilapia with Tomato Ragoût on Shredded Sweet Potatoes

———— Makes 4 servings ————

- 2 tablespoons all-purpose flour
- ¼ teaspoon red pepper flakes
- 4 tilapia fillets (about 1 pound)
- 2 tablespoons olive oil, divided
- 1 large sweet potato (12 ounces), peeled and shredded in food processor*
- ¼ teaspoon salt
  Black pepper (optional)

- 2 cloves garlic, minced
- ¼ cup diced red onion
- 1½ cups diced plum tomatoes (about 4)
- ¼ cup finely chopped fresh parsley
- 2 tablespoons capers, rinsed and drained

*One large sweet potato will make 3 cups shredded.

1. Combine flour and red pepper flakes in shallow dish; coat fish fillets with mixture.

2. Heat large nonstick skillet over medium-high heat. Add 1 tablespoon oil. Place fish in skillet; cook 4 to 6 minutes, carefully turning once, until fish flakes easily with fork. Remove from skillet; keep warm.

3. Meanwhile, bring 6 cups water to a boil in large saucepan. Add sweet potatoes and simmer about 5 minutes or until just tender. Drain. Add salt; season with black pepper, if desired.

4. Heat remaining 1 tablespoon oil in same skillet over medium-high heat. Add garlic and red onion; cook and stir 30 seconds. Add tomatoes, parsley and capers; heat through. Divide shredded potatoes among 4 plates; place tilapia on potatoes; top with tomato ragoût.

ON THE SIDE

Sweet & Savory Sweet Potato Salad

—— Makes 6 servings ——

4 cups peeled chopped cooked sweet potatoes (about 4 to 6)

¾ cup chopped green onions

½ cup chopped fresh parsley

½ cup dried unsweetened cherries

¼ cup plus 2 tablespoons rice wine vinegar

2 tablespoons coarse ground mustard

1 tablespoon extra virgin olive oil

¾ teaspoon garlic powder

¼ teaspoon black pepper

⅛ teaspoon salt

1. Combine sweet potatoes, green onions, parsley and cherries in large bowl; gently mix.

2. Whisk vinegar, mustard, oil, garlic powder, pepper and salt in small bowl until well blended. Pour over sweet potato mixture; gently toss to coat. Serve immediately or cover and refrigerate until ready to serve.

Vegetarian Rice Noodles

Makes 4 servings

½ cup soy sauce

⅓ cup sugar

¼ cup lime juice

2 fresh red Thai chiles *or* 1 large jalapeño pepper,* finely chopped

8 ounces thin rice noodles (rice vermicelli)

¼ cup vegetable oil

8 ounces firm tofu, drained and cut into triangles

1 jicama (8 ounces), peeled and chopped *or* 1 can (8 ounces) sliced water chestnuts, drained

2 medium sweet potatoes (1 pound), peeled and cut into ¼-inch-thick slices

2 large leeks, cut into ¼-inch-thick slices

¼ cup chopped unsalted dry-roasted peanuts

2 tablespoons chopped fresh mint

2 tablespoons chopped fresh cilantro

Chile peppers can sting and irritate the skin, so wear rubber gloves when handling peppers and do not touch your eyes.

1. Combine soy sauce, sugar, lime juice and chiles in small bowl until well blended; set aside.

2. Place rice noodles in medium bowl. Cover with hot water; let stand 15 minutes or until soft. Drain well; cut into 3-inch lengths.

3. Meanwhile, heat oil in large skillet over medium-high heat. Add tofu; stir-fry 4 minutes per side or until golden brown. Remove with slotted spatula to paper towel-lined baking sheet.

4. Add jicama to skillet; stir-fry 5 minutes or until lightly browned. Remove to baking sheet. Stir-fry sweet potatoes in batches until tender and browned; remove to baking sheet. Add leeks; stir-fry 1 minute; remove to baking sheet.

5. Stir soy sauce mixture; add to skillet. Heat until sugar dissolves. Add noodles; toss to coat. Gently stir in tofu, vegetables, peanuts, mint and cilantro.

Mashed
Sweet Potatoes & Parsnips
—————— Makes 6 servings ——————

2 large sweet potatoes (about 1¼ pounds), peeled and cut into 1-inch pieces

2 medium parsnips (about ½ pound), peeled and cut into ½-inch slices

¼ cup evaporated skimmed milk

1½ tablespoons butter or margarine

½ teaspoon salt

⅛ teaspoon ground nutmeg

¼ cup chopped fresh chives or green onions

1. Combine sweet potatoes and parsnips in large saucepan. Cover with cold water; bring to a boil over high heat. Reduce heat; simmer, uncovered, 15 minutes or until vegetables are tender.

2. Drain vegetables; return to pan. Add milk, butter, salt and nutmeg. Mash with potato masher over low heat until desired consistency is reached. Stir in chives.

Sweet Potato Fries

—— Makes 2 servings ——

1 large sweet potato (about 8 ounces)

2 teaspoons olive oil

¼ teaspoon coarse salt

¼ teaspoon black pepper

¼ teaspoon ground red pepper

Honey or maple syrup (optional)

1. Preheat oven to 425°F. Lightly spray baking sheet with nonstick cooking spray.

2. Peel sweet potato; cut lengthwise into long spears. Toss with oil, salt, black pepper and ground red pepper on prepared baking sheet. Arrange sweet potato spears in single layer not touching.

3. Bake 20 to 30 minutes or until lightly browned, turning halfway through baking time. Serve with honey, if desired.

Beer Batter Tempura

—— Makes 4 servings ——

1½ cups all-purpose flour
1½ cups Japanese beer, chilled
1 teaspoon salt
Dipping Sauce (recipe follows)
Vegetable oil for frying

½ pound green beans or asparagus tips
1 large sweet potato, cut into ¼-inch slices
1 medium eggplant, cut into ¼-inch slices

1. Combine flour, beer and salt in medium bowl just until mixed. Batter should be thin and lumpy. *Do not overmix.* Let stand 15 minutes. Meanwhile, prepare Dipping Sauce.

2. Heat 1 inch of oil in large saucepan to 375°F; adjust heat to maintain temperature.

3. Dip 10 to 12 green beans in batter; add to hot oil. Fry until light golden brown. Remove to wire racks or paper towels to drain; keep warm. Repeat with remaining vegetables, working with only one vegetable at a time and being careful not to crowd vegetables. Serve with Dipping Sauce.

Dipping Sauce

Makes about 1 cup

½ cup soy sauce
2 tablespoons rice wine
1 tablespoon sugar
½ teaspoon white vinegar

2 teaspoons minced fresh ginger
1 clove garlic, minced
2 green onions, thinly sliced

Combine soy sauce, rice wine, sugar and vinegar in small saucepan; cook and stir over medium heat 3 minutes or until sugar dissolves. Add ginger and garlic; cook and stir 2 minutes. Stir in green onions; remove from heat.

Spirited Sweet Potato Casserole

Makes 8 servings

2½ pounds sweet potatoes

2 tablespoons margarine

⅓ cup low-fat (1%) or fat-free (skim) milk

¼ cup packed brown sugar

2 tablespoons bourbon or apple juice

1 teaspoon ground cinnamon

1 teaspoon vanilla

2 egg whites

½ teaspoon salt

⅓ cup chopped pecans

3 whole pecans (optional)

1. Preheat oven to 375°F. Bake sweet potatoes 50 to 60 minutes or until very tender. Let stand 10 minutes to cool slightly. Leave oven on.

2. Scoop pulp from warm potatoes into large bowl; discard skins. Add margarine; mash with potato masher until smooth and margarine is melted. Stir in milk, brown sugar, bourbon, cinnamon and vanilla.

3. Beat egg whites in medium bowl with electric mixer at high speed until soft peaks form. Add salt; beat until stiff peaks form. Gently fold egg whites into sweet potato mixture.

4. Spray 1½-quart soufflé dish with nonstick cooking spray. Spoon sweet potato mixture into dish; sprinkle chopped pecans around edge of dish. Arrange whole pecans in center, if desired.

5. Bake 30 to 35 minutes or until soufflé is puffed and pecans are toasted. Serve immediately.

Quinoa & Roasted Vegetables

—————— Makes 6 servings ——————

2 medium sweet potatoes, cut into ½-inch-thick slices

1 medium eggplant, peeled and cut into ½-inch cubes

1 medium tomato, cut into wedges

1 large green bell pepper, sliced

1 small onion, cut into wedges

½ teaspoon salt

¼ teaspoon black pepper

¼ teaspoon ground red pepper

1 cup uncooked quinoa

2 cloves garlic, minced

½ teaspoon dried thyme

¼ teaspoon dried marjoram

2 cups water or fat-free reduced-sodium vegetable broth

1. Preheat oven to 450°F. Line large jelly-roll pan with foil; spray with nonstick cooking spray.

2. Combine sweet potatoes, eggplant, tomato, bell pepper and onion on prepared pan; spray lightly with cooking spray. Sprinkle with salt, black pepper and ground red pepper; toss to coat. Spread vegetables in single layer. Roast 20 to 30 minutes or until vegetables are browned and tender.

3. Meanwhile, place quinoa in fine-mesh strainer; rinse well under cold running water. Spray medium saucepan with cooking spray; heat over medium heat. Add garlic, thyme and marjoram; cook and stir 1 to 2 minutes. Add quinoa; cook and stir 2 to 3 minutes. Stir in water; bring to a boil over high heat. Reduce heat to low. Simmer, covered, 15 to 20 minutes or until water is absorbed. (Quinoa will appear somewhat translucent.) Transfer quinoa to large bowl; gently stir in roasted vegetables.

Two-Toned Stuffed Potatoes

—————— Makes 6 servings ——————

3 **large baking potatoes (12 ounces each)**

2 **large sweet potatoes (12 ounces each), dark flesh preferred**

3 **slices thick-cut bacon, cut in half crosswise diagonally**

2 **cups chopped onions**

⅔ **cup buttermilk**

¼ **cup (½ stick) butter, cut into small pieces**

¾ **teaspoon salt, divided**

1. Preheat oven to 450°F. Pierce potatoes with fork in several places. Bake directly on rack 45 minutes or until fork-tender. Let potatoes stand until cool enough to handle. *Reduce oven temperature to 350°F.*

2. Meanwhile, cook bacon in medium skillet over medium-high heat 6 to 8 minutes or until crisp. Remove from heat; transfer bacon to paper towels.

3. Add onions to drippings in skillet; cook about 12 minutes over medium-high heat or until golden brown. Remove onions from skillet; set aside. Stir buttermilk into skillet, scraping up any browned bits from bottom of pan. Add butter; stir until melted.

4. Cut baking potatoes in half lengthwise with serrated knife; scoop out flesh into large bowl. Reserve skins. Add three fourths buttermilk mixture, ½ teaspoon salt and three fourths onions to bowl. Mash with potato masher until smooth.

5. Cut sweet potatoes in half lengthwise with serrated knife; scoop out flesh into medium bowl. Discard skins. Add remaining one fourth buttermilk mixture, ¼ teaspoon salt and one fourth onions to sweet potatoes. Mash with potato masher until smooth.

6. Fill half of each reserved potato skin horizontally, vertically or diagonally with baked potato mixture; fill other half with sweet potato mixture. Top each stuffed potato half with bacon slice. Transfer stuffed potatoes to baking sheet; bake 15 minutes or until heated through.

Tip: These stuffed potatoes can be made and frozen weeks in advance. Reheat the frozen potatoes in a preheated 350°F oven for 75 to 90 minutes. If the potatoes are made ahead and refrigerated for a few days, reheat them in a preheated 350°F oven about 25 minutes.

SWEET ENDINGS

Sweet Potato Dump Cake

—— Makes 12 to 16 servings ——

1 can (29 ounces) sweet potatoes in light syrup, drained

1 package (about 15 ounces) yellow cake mix

3 eggs

1½ teaspoons apple pie spice, plus additional for top of cake

⅔ cup chopped nuts, divided

1. Preheat oven to 350°F. Spray 13×9-inch baking pan with nonstick cooking spray.

2. Place sweet potatoes in large bowl; mash with fork. Add cake mix, eggs and 1½ teaspoons apple pie spice; beat 1 to 2 minutes or until well blended. Stir in ⅓ cup nuts. Spread batter in prepared pan; sprinkle with remaining ⅓ cup nuts and additional apple pie spice.

3. Bake 30 to 35 minutes or until toothpick inserted into center comes out clean. Cool in pan at least 15 minutes before serving.

Sweet Potato & Pecan Casserole

—————— Makes 6 to 8 servings ——————

1 can (40 ounces) sweet
   potatoes, drained and mashed
½ cup apple juice
⅓ cup plus 2 tablespoons butter,
   melted, divided
½ teaspoon salt

½ teaspoon ground cinnamon
¼ teaspoon black pepper
2 eggs, beaten
⅓ cup chopped pecans
⅓ cup packed brown sugar
2 tablespoons all-purpose flour

Slow Cooker Directions

1. Lightly grease slow cooker. Combine sweet potatoes, apple juice, ⅓ cup butter, salt, cinnamon and pepper in large bowl. Beat in eggs. Place mixture into prepared slow cooker.

2. Combine pecans, brown sugar, flour and remaining 2 tablespoons butter in small bowl. Spread over sweet potatoes.

3. Cover; cook on HIGH 3 to 4 hours.

Tip: This casserole is excellent to make for the holidays. Using the slow cooker frees the oven for other dishes.

Sweet Potato Spice Whoopie Pies

Makes 22 whoopie pies

Cookies

1½ pounds sweet potatoes, quartered

1½ cups all-purpose flour

1¼ cups granulated sugar

2 teaspoons baking powder

1 teaspoon ground cinnamon

½ teaspoon baking soda

½ teaspoon salt

¼ teaspoon ground allspice

¾ cup canola oil

2 eggs

1 teaspoon vanilla

½ cup chopped walnuts

Filling

1 package (8 ounces) cream cheese, softened

¼ cup (½ stick) butter, softened

1½ cups powdered sugar

¼ teaspoon salt

¼ teaspoon vanilla

1. For cookies, place sweet potato in large saucepan; add enough water to cover. Cover and cook over medium heat 30 minutes or until fork-tender, adding additional water if necessary. Drain and set aside until cool enough to handle. Peel and mash sweet potatoes; measure 2 cups.

2. Preheat oven to 350°F. Line two cookie sheets with parchment paper. Sift flour, granulated sugar, baking powder, cinnamon, baking soda, ½ teaspoon salt and allspice into medium bowl.

3. Beat mashed sweet potatoes, oil, eggs and 1 teaspoon vanilla in large bowl with electric mixer at low speed until blended. Add flour mixture; beat at medium speed until well blended. Stir in walnuts. Drop rounded tablespoonfuls of batter 2 inches apart onto prepared cookie sheets.

4. Bake 10 to 12 minutes or until cookies spring back when lightly touched. Cool 2 minutes on cookie sheets. Remove to wire racks; cool completely.

5. For filling, beat cream cheese and butter in large bowl with electric mixer at medium speed until creamy. Add powdered sugar, ¼ teaspoon salt and ¼ teaspoon vanilla; beat until smooth.

6. Pipe or spread 2 tablespoons filling on flat side of half of cookies; top with remaining cookies.

Pecan-Crusted Sweet Potato Cheesecake

—— Makes 16 servings ——

Crust

- 1 cup finely crushed gingersnap cookies (about 20 [2-inch] cookies)
- ½ cup chopped pecans, toasted
- 5 tablespoons butter, melted
- 1 tablespoon sugar
- ⅛ teaspoon salt

Filling

- 4 packages (8 ounces each) cream cheese, softened
- 1 can (15 ounces) sweet potatoes in syrup, drained
- 1¼ cups sugar
- 1 cup whipping cream
- 3 eggs
- 2 teaspoons vanilla
- ½ to 1 tablespoon pumpkin pie spice

Whipped cream and pecan halves

1. Preheat oven to 350°F. Lightly coat 10-inch springform pan with nonstick cooking spray. Wrap double layer of heavy-duty foil around outside of pan.

2. Combine cookies, chopped pecans, butter, sugar and salt in food processor or blender; pulse until coarse crumbs form. Press crumbs evenly into bottom (not side) of prepared pan. Bake 8 minutes; remove to wire rack to cool slightly.

3. Combine cream cheese, sweet potatoes, sugar, cream, eggs, vanilla and pumpkin pie spice in food processor or blender; process until smooth. Pour into crust. Place springform pan in larger roasting pan or broiler pan; add enough hot water to come one third of the way up side of springform pan.

4. Bake 1½ hours or until slightly puffed, softly set and top is golden. Remove to wire rack to cool completely. Cover and refrigerate overnight. Top with whipped cream and pecan halves, if desired.

Sweet Potato Crumb Cake

———— Makes 6 cakes ————

Crumb

- ½ cup sugar
- Grated peel of 1 orange
- 1 teaspoon ground cinnamon
- ½ cup chopped pecans
- ¼ cup all-purpose flour
- ¼ cup old-fashioned oats
- ¼ cup (½ stick) cold butter, cut into 4 pieces

Cake

- 1 package (16 ounces) sweet potato pound cake mix, plus ingredients to prepare mix
- Powdered sugar (optional)

1. Preheat oven to 350°F. Spray six individual loaf pans with nonstick cooking spray.*

2. Combine sugar and orange peel in food processor; pulse using on/off action, several times to thoroughly mix. Add cinnamon and pecans; pulse until pecans are size of peas. Reserve ⅓ cup of crumb mixture; set aside.

3. Add flour, oats and butter to remaining crumb mixture in food processor; pulse until mixture resembles coarse crumbs.

4. Prepare cake mix according to package directions. Divide batter in half. Evenly pour one half into prepared pans. Evenly sprinkle with ⅓ cup reserved crumb mixture. Spoon remaining batter evenly over crumb mixture. Top with oat crumb mixture.

5. Bake 25 to 30 minutes or until toothpick inserted into middle comes out clean. Cool in pans 15 minutes. Remove to wire rack; cool completely. Dust with powdered sugar, if desired.

We used a 6-loaf mini loaf pan with removable bottoms in each section. Eight muffin cups (in a standard, 12-cup muffin tin) can be used instead.

INDEX

METRIC CONVERSION CHART

VOLUME MEASUREMENTS (dry)

$\frac{1}{8}$ teaspoon = 0.5 mL
$\frac{1}{4}$ teaspoon = 1 mL
$\frac{1}{2}$ teaspoon = 2 mL
$\frac{3}{4}$ teaspoon = 4 mL
1 teaspoon = 5 mL
1 tablespoon = 15 mL
2 tablespoons = 30 mL
$\frac{1}{4}$ cup = 60 mL
$\frac{1}{3}$ cup = 75 mL
$\frac{1}{2}$ cup = 125 mL
$\frac{2}{3}$ cup = 150 mL
$\frac{3}{4}$ cup = 175 mL
1 cup = 250 mL
2 cups = 1 pint = 500 mL
3 cups = 750 mL
4 cups = 1 quart = 1 L

VOLUME MEASUREMENTS (fluid)

1 fluid ounce (2 tablespoons) = 30 mL
4 fluid ounces ($\frac{1}{2}$ cup) = 125 mL
8 fluid ounces (1 cup) = 250 mL
12 fluid ounces (1$\frac{1}{2}$ cups) = 375 mL
16 fluid ounces (2 cups) = 500 mL

WEIGHTS (mass)

$\frac{1}{2}$ ounce = 15 g
1 ounce = 30 g
3 ounces = 90 g
4 ounces = 120 g
8 ounces = 225 g
10 ounces = 285 g
12 ounces = 360 g
16 ounces = 1 pound = 450 g

DIMENSIONS

$\frac{1}{16}$ inch = 2 mm
$\frac{1}{8}$ inch = 3 mm
$\frac{1}{4}$ inch = 6 mm
$\frac{1}{2}$ inch = 1.5 cm
$\frac{3}{4}$ inch = 2 cm
1 inch = 2.5 cm

OVEN TEMPERATURES

250°F = 120°C
275°F = 140°C
300°F = 150°C
325°F = 160°C
350°F = 180°C
375°F = 190°C
400°F = 200°C
425°F = 220°C
450°F = 230°C

BAKING PAN SIZES

Utensil	Size in Inches/Quarts	Metric Volume	Size in Centimeters
Baking or Cake Pan (square or rectangular)	8×8×2	2 L	20×20×5
	9×9×2	2.5 L	23×23×5
	12×8×2	3 L	30×20×5
	13×9×2	3.5 L	33×23×5
Loaf Pan	8×4×3	1.5 L	20×10×7
	9×5×3	2 L	23×13×7
Round Layer Cake Pan	8×1½	1.2 L	20×4
	9×1½	1.5 L	23×4
Pie Plate	8×1¼	750 mL	20×3
	9×1¼	1 L	23×3
Baking Dish or Casserole	1 quart	1 L	—
	1½ quart	1.5 L	—
	2 quart	2 L	—